HOME ALONE™

SURVIVAL

GUIDE

JANE HAMMERSLOUGH

A TRUMPET CLUB ORIGINAL BOOK

HEY YOU—THAT'S *MY* BOOK!!

    I'M GOING TO GIVE YOU TILL THE COUNT OF TEN TO GET YOUR UGLY, YELLOW, NO-GOOD KEYSTER OFF MY PROPERTY!!! LEAVE IT ON THE DOORSTEP AND GET OUT! (THANKS A LOT!!)

THIS BOOK BELONGS TO:

Name _____

Address _____

_____

Telephone _____

INTRODUCTION BY KEVIN McCALLISTER

Did you ever wish your whole family would *disappear*? Well, *I* did once, and when I woke up one day, they were gone! We were all supposed to go to France, but I got left behind by mistake. And one time, my mom, dad, brothers, sisters, cousins, uncle and aunt disappeared when I actually *wanted* to be with them. They all went to Florida for Christmas vacation while I ended up staying by myself at the Plaza Hotel in New York City—it was quite a trip!

Some folks made a few movies about what happened to me while I was all alone. If you saw them, you know that being at home alone was really fun for me at times. Being alone with all the hotel room service I wanted was even better!

The best part about being all by myself was getting to do what *I* wanted. I could watch any video I wanted, and I could eat a whole cheese pizza without sharing it with *anyone*. Oh yeah, I almost forgot—my rotten older brother Buzz wasn't around to bug me. (Maybe *that* was the best part!)

But being alone can get scary. And sometimes it gets really boring and lonely. Believe it or not, I even started to *miss* my family!

If you've ever spent time alone the way I did, you know that it can sometimes be serious as well as fun. You probably won't ever need to dodge Harry and Marv, the dopey Wet Bandits, the way I did. But you still have to *survive* a lot of things when your mom and dad aren't around. That's where this book comes in handy.

What do you do if someone comes to the door when you are at home alone? How do you stay safe when you are out by yourself? What do you do if your brother or sister is driving you *nuts*? (Believe me, I know all about *that*.) And what about if you're scared, the way I was sometimes when I was alone? Or what if you're just TOTALLY bored?

This book can give you ideas for things to do to survive when you're at home—or away from home—alone. (It can also give you ideas on things *not* to do, like sledding down your stairs the way I did—oops!)

It's also got lots of funny stories and photos from *Home Alone 2: Lost in New York* to remind you of what it was like for *me* when I was alone in my second movie on the streets of New York.

Hey, *you* can survive being at home alone or alone on the road, the way I did. Once you get the hang of it, it's easy. Good luck—and don't do anything I wouldn't do!

Kevin

HOT LINES

Mom's work phone _____
Dad's work phone _____
Neighbors I Can Count On_____
_____
_____

Fire Department _____
Police _____
Ambulance _____
Family Doctor _____
Emergency Medical
Service _____
Poison Control/Nearest
Hospital _____
IN MANY AREAS, YOU CAN ALSO DIAL 911 OR 0 FOR OPERATOR
FOR ALL EMERGENCIES

FILL IN *YOUR* IMPORTANT NUMBERS HERE:
_____
_____
_____
_____

GETTING HOME

What do you do if you're walking home, minding your own business, and someone you don't know is following you?

Think fast! Like Kevin, you can make a run for it.... Dodge around crowds of people, do a wild skid across a packed ice-skating rink, and leap over snowbanks the way Kevin does when he accidentally steals a tooth-brush, and needs to get away—*fast*.

But just when he thinks the worst is over, Kevin runs smack into Harry and Marv, the mean "Wet Bandits" who are plotting to break into his house. As he walks along, Kevin knows their van is right behind him, and they're just waiting for him to go home—*alone*. How does he outwit them?

Kevin disappears into thin air! Not really, but he *does* disappear into a Christmas nativity scene right outside his church. With a little ingenuity, Kevin quickly dis-guises himself as a statue of a shepherd. Marv and Harry don't notice him, and they drive right past!

Another time, when he is in New York City by himself,

Kevin loses Harry and Marv by creating a big distraction. He makes a pretty woman on the street think that Marv has pinched her. She is outraged! Kevin quickly escapes the huge fight that follows and runs into the park. For the moment, anyway, he's safe from the thieves!!

What do you do if you think someone is following you? Do you pinch someone to attract attention, and blame it on the person who is following you? Do you throw yourself, face first, into a snowbank and hope no one notices you? Or do you disappear by doing a quick-change disguise, like Kevin?

No, you don't do *any* of these things!! Chances are that you won't be able to turn yourself into a shepherd (or even a sheep) in an instant, the way Kevin did. And pinching a stranger to attract attention could prove hazardous to your health!

Still, you *can* do some things to get home safely:

- Starting now, figure out the most direct route home from school. It has to be on *main* roads—no short-cuts through deserted or dangerous areas.
- Keep away from areas that aren't familiar to you. (The point is to get home, *not* to get lost!)
- If a stranger in a car calls you over to ask for directions, don't get too close. You don't know who the person is, or what they really want. They can always talk to an adult instead. (After all, they might turn out to be like Harry and Marv....)
- Watch out for traffic!! Kevin almost gets whomped by the burglars' van when he isn't paying attention on his way home.

Here's what you can do if you think someone is following you:

- Just like Kevin did, start walking faster or running, if you can. If you think a car is following you, walk in the other direction so the car will have to turn around too.
- Make it seem like you are not alone. Strike up a conversation with a passerby. Or, if no one's around, talk to an "imaginary friend." Talk to a whole *crowd* of imaginary friends. Pretend you see people you know, and wave or call out. (People may think you're crazy, but you'll be safer!)
- Cross the street.
- Go to a police or fire station or a store to ask for help or go into a friendly neighbor's house. (Make sure you and your parents know them before you show up at their door.)
- If you still think someone is following you when you reach your house, don't go in. Go to a neighbor's or a friend's house instead, and call a parent. (You can also go to a church or another public building, the way Kevin did.)

Don't ever get into the car of someone that you don't know, even if *they* know *your* name. Even though Marv says that kids are stupid and will believe anything, *you* know better. And even if the person tells you that they know your parents, tell them you'd rather walk. When your parents come home, ask them about that person.

Did someone break into your house while you were at school? If you think so, don't go inside. Some bur-

Starting now, figure out the direct route home from school.

glaries are obvious. Look at the Wet Bandits—they left water running at every house they robbed. If you see water spilling out of your kitchen door—definitely do not go in!!

But not all robbers are as dumb as Harry and Marv. Sometimes break-ins are harder to spot. Signs of a robbery might include windows that are broken, doors that are left open, and ladders that are propped up against your house. If you see any of these things, go to a neighbor's house and call a parent or the police.

Talk It Over

Some places have Neighborhood Watch areas. Houses that are part of this program have Neighborhood Watch stickers in their windows. If you are scared for any reason, you can ring the doorbells at these houses. Ask your parents about the Neighborhood Watch area in your neighborhood. Look for the Neighborhood Watch stickers on houses so you'll always know a place you can get help when you're out alone.

Make sure that you talk with your parents about other people that you can contact in an emergency. It pays to be prepared!

It's Key

Kevin is good at hiding the fact that he's home alone from people in stores, neighbors, the police—even from Marv and Harry, for a while. You should learn how to do this too.

Keep your house key out of sight when you're not using it. Leave it inside a pocket or bag, on a chain, tucked inside your clothes. Don't lend it to anyone and don't put your name or address on it.

Sit down with your parents and figure out which of your neighbors should have a spare key, in case you lose yours. Agree on someone who is usually home when you are, and make sure it's someone *you* like. (Don't pick anyone who gives you the creeps!)

Make sure you know your parents' daytime phone numbers by heart. If you lose your key and can't get a spare, call a parent from a neighbor's house or a pay phone. Carry an emergency quarter with you.

Do you have a plan for what you would do if you were locked out of your house? Where's *your* spare key? Be sure you know how to find it.

Lock up

When you get home, lock the doors to your house, and *keep them locked* while you are at home alone.

If you lose your key and can't get a spare, call a parent
from a neighbor's house or a pay phone.

ARE YOU IN THE HOUSE ALONE?

What do you do if you're home alone, and someone you don't know comes to your door?

A) You run like crazy, screaming at the top of your lungs, and dive onto your parents' bed.

B) You run like crazy up to your parents' room, dive *under* the bed, then tell yourself you're a wimp for hiding.

C) Hidden from sight, you start a video at the part where the tough guy says, "You got to the count of ten to get your lousy, lying, low-down, four-flushing carcass out that door!"

D) You stage a "shadow" party, complete with wildly dancing couples, loud music and a "waiter" passing out drinks and food—with you as the only *real* guest.

E) All of the above.

If you're like Kevin, you chose **E**—all of the above. He avoids talking to *everyone*: burglars, crazed hotel workers, pizza delivery guys, *and* the police who want to help him.

You, on the other hand, may not want to avoid all of the people that show up at your door when you are at home alone. And even Kevin soon realizes that hiding *all* of the time is silly, not safe. As he tells himself after a few minutes of hiding, "This is ridiculous. Only a wimp would be hiding under a bed. And I can't be a wimp—I'm the man of the house!"

When you're alone at home, you are the man—or woman—of the house! What do you do when there's a stranger at the door?

First, when someone comes to your house, keep the door locked and find out who it is. If you have a peephole, look through it. (Remember how Kevin secretly looks out to discover that it is Marv and Harry at the door?)

Find out what the person wants. Act as if your mom and dad are there, and call out to them. Then tell the person, "My mom and dad can't come to the door right now. Can I leave a message for you?"

Talk with your parents about what you should do if a delivery person will be arriving. You and your parents might decide that you should tell the delivery person to leave the package outside on the doorstep, the way Kevin did with his pizza. (Although he almost scared the delivery guy to death when he used his video "voice"!) You might also ask the person to leave the package with a neighbor who you and your parents know and trust.

You and your parents might also decide that you can open the door and take the package yourself. Check out the person *before* you unlock and open the door. Is he or she wearing an official-looking uniform? Remember how official Harry looked in his fake policeman's uniform? Use your best judgment. And always make sure it's okay with your parents before you open the door to *anyone* you don't know.

What if someone unexpectedly arrives at your house like a repair person or a delivery person? (Harry and Marv looked like real plumbers when they drove around Kevin's neighborhood, deciding which house to rob first!) Keep your door *locked*, and ask the person to wait a moment. Then call a parent to find out what to do.

Because Kevin was left alone by mistake, he didn't know how to reach his parents. But most of the time, you will be able to reach yours. If you *can't* reach a parent, *don't* open the door. *Don't* say you are home alone. Tell the person at the door to come back to the house another time.

If a stranger at the door tells you it's an emergency and they need to use the phone right away, tell them *you'll* make the call for them, or tell them to go to a neighbor's house. Make sure they *stay* outside of your house. (It may sound mean, but you'll be safe in case they're like the Wet Bandits.) And remember—*always* keep *all* doors locked.

Telephone

After Kevin's family accidentally left him behind when they went to France, they couldn't reach him. Why? Because a storm had knocked out the telephone service in the whole area! The police couldn't reach Kevin, and neither could his parents. In fact, no one was really sure that Kevin *was* at home—and for a long time, he hides the fact that he is at home *alone.*

Just like Kevin, *you* should keep it to yourself that your parents aren't around when you're at home alone. When someone calls on the phone for a parent, you can say, "My mom and dad can't come to the phone right now. Who's calling, please?"

If you don't know the caller very well, and he or she starts asking a lot of questions about when your mom or dad will be available, don't give out too much information. If it sounds very important, call one of your parents and let them know about the call as soon as possible. Keep a notepad by the phone so you can write down messages.

Have you ever gotten a *weird* phone call? People hanging up, breathing, and even wrong numbers can be scary if you are alone. If you ever get a call that is scary or threatening, you should hang up right away. If your family has an answering machine, turn it on and let the machine answer the calls. This may help the problem. *Don't* take the phone off the hook, in case your parents need to reach you.

We're Having a Party!

With a little creativity, Kevin was able to take a few household objects, hook them up just right, and transform them into a party full of people! At least, it *looked* that way....

And when he was staying by himself at the Plaza, Kevin was able to scare a snooping concierge *witless* with an inflatable rubber clown! Kevin rigged up a "man" in his shower who shouted, "Get out of here ... or I'll come out and slap you silly!" The concierge ran out of Kevin's suite faster than you could say "Room Service"!

Both times, Kevin fooled the bad guys and made them think that he was not alone. By making life-size, people-shaped shadows, Kevin convinced the Wet Bandits and others that there were people at home with him. Kevin even made the shadows move, like the dancing "guests" at the party, or the "man" showering in the hotel. Using a tape recorder and a VCR, he made his shadow people "talk."

You can have fun making shadows with things you find around the house, the way Kevin did. And you may even fool someone into thinking that you have other people at home with you! Anyway, you're sure to have fun. Here's how:

- Start by experimenting. Turn on a light or a flashlight in a room, and try standing various distances from it, holding your object in the light to create a shadow. You can experiment with different objects—try using model dinosaurs, "micromachines," or action fig-ures—to make larger-than-life shadows. The closer you are to the light, the larger and darker the shadow will be.
- To make your shadows look like Kevin's "party" or "shower man," you'll need larger objects. Remember how Kevin uses an inflatable clown to fool the con-cierge? Or the large cutout of the basketball player that looks like a waiter at the shadow party? Check around your house for an object that might cast a shadow that looks like something else. You can

even start with an old pillow for a body and attach cardboard-tube arms and legs. Make a head out of a rubber ball, and add a hat!

• Once you have your shadow figure, you need to think about where to put it. Kevin's "party" takes place behind closed curtains in his living room, and a closed shower curtain makes the concierge think that there's really a person in the bathroom. Find a place where you can close curtains to set the stage for your shadow show.

• At the Plaza, Kevin makes his "shadow man" move by attaching a piece of string to him and tugging on it. Try to see if you can move your own creation this way. (Make sure you don't block the shadow yourself!)

Sound Effects

"Keep the change, you filthy animal," a tough-sounding voice tells the guy who delivers a pizza to Kevin's house. Was there really a gangster inside? No—it was only Kevin and his VCR!

And armed with only his tape recorder, Kevin makes a whole crowd of people at the hotel believe that a dangerous gangster is in his room!

You can have fun with sound effects the way Kevin does. Start by closing your eyes and listening to your favorite videos. Do the characters say things that might scare people away? Do you hear things that sound funny if you can't see the picture? (Hint: The sound track from *Bambi, The Three Little Pigs,* and *Cinderella* might not work as well as some other videos!)

You can play back your favorite parts, just like Kevin

did. Or you can record parts of television shows and movies with your VCR. You can also try to make your own special sound effects. Remember when Kevin grosses out his cousins and sister with the disgusting noises that he records? Yuck!

Here are some ideas for sounds to record:

* loud barking dogs
* sirens
* the dialogue from a movie or television show when the police say, "You're under arrest!"
* a big car crash
* a big party
* lots of people laughing
* a scary laugh
* a dog howling
* really bad singing (like Uncle Frank's!)

You can play back the sounds if you want to scare someone away, or if you just want to play a joke on someone. (Don't do anything mean, though.) Use your imagination!

ARE YOUR BROTHERS AND/OR SISTERS (COUSINS, NEIGHBORS OR ASSORTED OTHER KIDS) DRIVING YOU CRAZY?

Let's face facts here. Sometimes your brothers, sisters, and other kids are okay. But sometimes they act like total jerks! And sometimes you're stuck with them, even if you'd much rather be at home alone.

Stuff To Do With Younger Brothers and Sisters

When your younger brothers or sisters are driving you up a wall, do you:

A) Hang them upside down until your parents get home.

B) Run away from home yourself.

C) Admit defeat and try to have fun with them.

If you chose **C**, congratulations! Even though answers **A** and **B** might sound good, they could lead to lots of, uh, problems. Besides, torturing your brother or sister takes too much time, and running away from home takes too much effort. And really—why should you let your rotten little brother or sister make you leave *your* home!

All in all, it's a better idea to try having fun with the little monsters. You might even have a good time! As the old saying goes: If you can't beat 'em, join 'em!

Should you hang your brother or sister upside down? Absolutely not!

So what do you with the rug rats? Even Kevin knows that watching too much TV gets really boring. But even the littlest kid will enjoy playing Concentration with an ordinary deck of cards. Here's how:

- Lay all the cards in the deck facedown on the floor (spread out so they're not in a pile).
- Turn over cards, two at a time. If the two cards don't make a pair, turn them facedown again.
- Try to remember where each card is. The goal is to turn over pairs. If you turn over a pair of cards, it is yours to keep, and you get to go again.
- The person who has the most pairs of cards at the end of the game wins.

You can show your little brothers and sisters how to do easy art projects like these:

"Recycle Art" Collages
Tear interesting shapes from cardboard, plastic, fabric, and aluminum foil throw-away items. Try to use lots of different colors and textures. (You can make greeting cards by folding the paper in half first.)

Paper Bag Fish
Hold the open end of a small paper bag bunched up together and blow air into it. Fasten the end with a string or rubber band so it's like a paper balloon. Draw a fish face on the bottom of the bag, and fins on the sides.

Rock Paperweights
Find and wash small smooth rocks. Paint or draw designs on them.

"Handmade" Giant Soap Bubble Blower

Mix three tablespoons of dishwashing detergent with a cup of water in a bowl. Tell your brother or sister to make an O-shape with their hands, dip them into the bubble solution, and blow. Instant giant bubbles! (Do this activity outside.)

Soap "Crayons"

For each color, mix one cup of soap flakes with a tablespoon of hot water. Add ten drops of food color—more if you want darker colors. Stir the mixture until it thickens. (It takes a long time!) With a spoon, press the mixture into an empty ice-cube tray or a Styrofoam egg carton. Let the soap crayons dry for a day or two.

OH, THE PAIN OF IT...

Uh oh. What if you're babysitting or home alone with a friend and someone skins a knee? Or gets a nosebleed. Or bumps his head. What do you do?

If you think the problem is at all serious, call a parent. But if it's minor, you can practice some basic first aid! Ask your parents to show you where the first-aid items are kept and show you how to use them. Here are some ways to treat minor accidents:

Small Cuts and Scratches
- Wash the cut with lots of soap and water. Let the skin dry.
- Apply first-aid cream if you have it.
- Cover with a bandage.

Nosebleeds
- Tell the person to sit up and lean forward slightly. *Don't* let him or her lie down.
- Pinch the nose *gently* for a few minutes.

• Put a cool, wet cloth on the person's nose and face. Tell the person not to blow his (or her) nose.

Bumps
• Make an ice pack by wrapping ice cubes in a clean cloth.
• Hold the ice pack on the place you bumped.

HOME SAFETY: TAKE CHARGE!

A burglar is about to break into the McCallister house. He reaches out to turn the doorknob and *YOW!!!*—it's flaming hot! Later, his hair gets burned off, he gets clonked in the head with a flying paint can, and—CUT!!

Hey, folks, it's only a movie!

You probably never will have to ward off burglars in the wild ways that Kevin did. Still, as Kevin tells himself when he's at home alone, "This is *my* house. I must defend it!" He takes charge to keep his home safe. And in real life, you can too. But how?

Remember how Kevin sets up a trap for the Wet Bandits with his small cars and trucks? They slip and fall on their faces! And remember what happens in New York when Kevin throws down a bunch of little beads in the robbers' path? It's funny to watch the expressions on Marv and Harry's faces when they skid like crazy!

But in real life, the same things that trip up the robbers can trip *you* up as well. Kevin's dad is right when he asks Kevin to move his "micromachines." Stay safe and put away marbles, cars, and other small toys when you're not using them.

Spills and broken glass can be dangerous as well. Even though it's funny to watch Kevin trick Marv into crunching his bare foot down on a bunch of Christmas-tree ornaments, it wouldn't be too funny if it happened to *you*.

If you spill something, wipe it up right away so nobody slips. And if you break a glass, make sure you are wearing shoes before you try to clean it up. Keep cats and dogs away, so they don't hurt *their* feet. Carefully sweep up the large pieces of glass into a dustpan, then pour them into a paper bag. Look around to make sure you haven't missed any! Close up the paper bag and put it in the garbage. Use a bunch of wet paper towels to wipe up the rest of the tiny glass pieces. Then rinse your hands.

When he's at home alone, Kevin discovers that his brother Buzz's room is filled with all kinds of interesting things. Unfortunately, he also discovers that *climbing* shelves to find something can be disastrous! (Remember how everything comes crashing down?) If you need to get something on a high shelf, use a stepladder to reach it.

Wouldn't it be great if you could call room service whenever you felt like eating something, the way Kevin did when he was staying by himself at the Plaza? When he was by himself at home though, Kevin knew how to use his family's microwave to cook dinner for himself.

Do you know how to use the microwave, washing machine, and other appliances? Talk it over with your parents. Are you allowed to use these things at home?

If you are, you should learn how to use them the right way, so you won't have any accidents. Don't experiment if you aren't sure how they work—you might break them, and you could get hurt!

HOME ALONE™ BATTLE PLAN #1: OPERATION HOME SAFETY

Kevin's mission is to protect his home. To prepare for the Wet Bandits, he writes up a Battle Plan. *You* can protect your home—and yourself—by creating a Battle Plan to make your house safe.

You can carry out Operation Home Safety on a Saturday. Enlist a parent to work with you, but *you* must be the expert. Here's how:

Walk around the house with one of your parents. Use the following checklist as a guide to find things that might not be safe in your house:

- Test to see if smoke alarms work.
- Make sure electrical cords are not frayed.
- Make sure all electrical wires are out of the way, so you can't trip on them.
- Keep cleaning products, plant food, medicines, etc., out of reach of animals and small brothers and sisters—they might eat them.
- Keep paper, pot holders, and trash away from the stove so you don't accidentally set them on fire.

- Make sure wastebaskets are far away from space heaters so they don't accidentally catch on fire.
- Check windows and locks to make sure they are secure and are working properly.

HOME ALONE™ BATTLE PLAN #2: OPERATION FIRE ESCAPE

Even if *your* family is so annoying that it makes Uncle Frank, cousin Fuller, and brother Buzz look like a barrel of monkeys, you must *still* sit down together and talk about what everyone should do if there's a fire. And again, you can look smart because *you* have the all-important Battle Plan checklist:

- Talk about how to get out of each room in your house in case of fire. Each room should have two ways of escape.
- Make sure *every* person in your family knows how to get out of each room.
- Arrange for a place *outside* of your house for your family to meet when you leave your house.
- Stage a fire drill with your entire family.
- Talk about different kinds of fires, and what to do for each. Ask your parents what you should do differently if there's a grease fire or an electrical fire.
- Everyone should learn the STOP, DROP, and ROLL rule. If you or your clothes are on fire, STOP moving

and cover your face with your hands. Then DROP, face forward, to the ground. ROLL back and forth on the floor to beat out the flames. Everyone should practice STOP, DROP, and ROLL until it becomes automatic.

CREATE AN EMERGENCY SURVIVAL KIT

Kevin ended up staying at home alone all because the electricity in his house went out in the middle of the night. What if the electricity goes out when you are at home alone?

If there's a blackout, do *you* know where the flashlight is? You can be prepared for weather emergencies like snow or rain storms by making an Emergency Survival Kit.

Use a shoe box to store all the items you'll need. Decorate the outside of the box and label it in bright red letters. Make sure it is stored in an easy-to-find place, and tell everyone in your family where it is. You might want to include:

* a flashlight
* extra batteries
* a transistor radio
* bandages
* a bottle of water
* small games

* a deck of cards
* an extra copy of *The Home Alone*™ *Survival Guide*!

You're never too old to be afraid.

IF YOU HAVE THE CREEPS...

"You're never too old to be afraid." That's what Marley, the old man who lives next door in *Home Alone™*, tells Kevin. And he's right. Everyone feels scared sometimes, especially when left alone.

Is your house filled with strange noises? Did you ever think that someone was trying to get into your house? Do you ever think that someone or something might be hiding in a closet? Is there some place in your house that gives you the creeps?

For Kevin, that place is the basement. It's dark and smells strange. It has all kinds of weird old stuff around. He imagines that the noisy furnace down there is some kind of horrible, hungry monster with a big, fiery mouth. *AUUGGHHHH!!!* Every time Kevin has to go down to the basement, he's terrified.

But once Kevin spends some time in the basement, he stops feeling afraid. He realizes that the furnace is just a furnace, and it happens to make weird noises. He stops imagining that it is a scary, crazed creature. He even tells the boiler to shut up. As Kevin tells Marley, when he gets used to the boiler, he stops being afraid of it.

What makes *you* feel afraid? Write down the things that make you scared when you are home alone:

_____

_____

_____

_____

Are you worried about someone breaking into your house?

Start Sleuthing!

If something is unusual or unfamiliar, it can be scary. Like Kevin, you can start to think about all sorts of bad things. But you can *also* stop scary thoughts by learning more about the things that scare you.

Look over your list of things that scare you. You can handle whatever makes you afraid, with a little detective work. Here's how:

- Is there a sound that makes you afraid? You may hear something and imagine bad things. Close your eyes and listen to the sounds around your house. Identify the sounds of appliances, dogs barking, the wind outside, banging pipes, dripping faucets, and other normal household noises. Can you figure out what makes the sound that scared you? (Do this with a parent if you still aren't sure what is causing the scary noise.)
- Is there a place in your house that's creepy? Check out the place with a parent. Become familiar with it. Think about *exactly* what is in that place. Spend time in that place, if you can.
- Does darkness make you nervous? Turn on lights. Use a flashlight to look in shadowy areas if you think something is there.
- Are you worried about someone breaking into your house? Look around your house with a parent, and learn how the locks on the doors and windows work.
- Is there a neighbor or some other person who makes you nervous? Why? Ask a parent about that person. (Remember the bad stories Kevin heard about Marley? It turned out that they weren't true.)

- Talking over your fears with someone can help. List six people to call if you are afraid:

NAME   TELEPHONE

1. _____
2. _____
3. _____
4. _____
5. _____
6. _____

Look at your list of fears again. In the space below, write down each fear. Now write down the "detective work" that you can do to help get over your fear:

FEAR   WHAT I CAN DO ABOUT IT

_____
_____
_____
_____
_____
_____
_____
_____

Take your mind off feeling scared by using your imagination:

- Close your eyes, and imagine your favorite place in the entire world. Imagine that you are there, and you can do anything you want. What would you do in your favorite place?

- What would Kevin do if he were in your shoes? Think about how he would handle being alone and afraid in *your* house.
- Re-read a favorite, familiar book. (Don't pick a scary one!) Or think of a character from a book you like a lot. Imagine that you are that character. Instead of being at home alone, what would you be doing?
- Make a list of things you want to do over the next week, and then do one of those things.
- Are you interested in knowing more about a particular subject? Find a book on that subject in your local library or school and read it.

STREET SMARTS: SURVIVING WHEN YOU'RE OUT AND ABOUT BY YOURSELF

Okay—even little kids know that you're not supposed to cross the street when the light is red. And even *dummies* know that you shouldn't take candy from strangers.

But sometimes when you're out by yourself the rules aren't so clear. Sometimes it's hard to know just what to do to stay safe. That's where your "street smarts" come in.

When Kevin goes to the supermarket to shop for food, he uses his street smarts when the girl at the checkout counter questions him. He says that his mom is waiting out in the car, but the girl is still suspicious. She asks where he lives. "I can't tell you that," says Kevin. "Why?" she asks, even more suspicious. "You're a stranger," replies Kevin, and smiles.

The girl is surprised by Kevin's answer. She doesn't expect him to act so sure of himself. When you're out by yourself, you can do the same thing.

Like Kevin, don't let *anyone* know that you're by yourself at a mall, on the street, or in a store. If anyone asks you where your parents are, tell them that they are waiting for you nearby. (And remember to sound *sure of yourself*, not wimpy!!) If they ask where you live, tell them you aren't allowed to tell strangers anything like that. (If you want, you can act surprised that they would even ask!)

Kevin is street smart when he is out and about in New York City—most of the time. But remember when he starts to space out? It happens when he is standing on the sidewalk, not paying attention to anything except fooling around with a magnifying glass and a map of the city. It's the perfect opportunity for the Wet Bandits to snag him!!

The key to having street smarts is to keep your eyes open and to think fast. Be aware of what is happening around you. Don't be a "space cadet."

Kevin also acts like a space cadet when he is at the airport with his family, getting ready to go to Florida. That's the whole reason he ends up in New York! Kevin is looking down, trying to fix his mini tape recorder, while he is walking along in the airport. He doesn't realize that his whole family is headed in a completely different direction!

When he finally *does* look ahead of him, he sees a man in a raincoat that looks just like his dad. Not paying much attention, he follows the man onto a plane. Oh, no! It's not his dad and it's not the plane for Florida!

As it turns out in the movie, Kevin has some great adventures in New York City. (How many kids end up traveling by themselves to the Plaza Hotel? And how many kids get to use their dad's credit card as much as they want?!) But in real life, not paying attention when you're out can get you into real trouble.

Even though the pigeon lady turned out to be a nice
stranger...

...some strangers aren't so nice. In the movies...
and in real life...be careful.

Pay Attention!

If you see someone who is acting weird, move away. If you are following someone, like when Kevin *thinks* he's following his dad, make sure it's really *him*, and not some guy who has the same raincoat.

And remember—when you're out by yourself, always carry a couple of emergency quarters. (No, not for the video arcade, dummy!) Make sure that you can always call a parent if you need to.

Most people are pretty nice, but not everyone is.

Strangers

Most people are pretty nice. Most wouldn't think of bothering a kid who is out without his or her parents. But not everyone is like that.

Sometimes, the way someone looks can fool you. Remember how much the Pigeon Lady scares Kevin when he first sees her? And remember Marley, with his big black boots and snow shovel that makes a horrible *scr-r-r-aping* sound? Both the Pigeon Lady and Marley turn out to be great people and they help Kevin a lot.

On the other hand, remember when Marv first comes to Kevin's house? He's dressed up like a police officer, and seems like he wants to help the McCallisters by keeping an eye on their house while they are away on vacation. He is very friendly to Kevin. But *you* know what happens later!

Of course, in real life, most police officers are not robbers in disguise. If you need help when you are out alone, you can ask a police officer.

If other people speak with you when you are out by yourself, use your street smarts. Are they asking things you shouldn't answer? Or are they just being friendly? Pay attention. Like Kevin, you never know when good— or bad—things can happen. Staying alert can help make good things happen more often than not.

ARE YOU *TOTALLY* BORED?

AUGGGHHHH! There's *nothing* to do!

Are you ever *totally* bored when you are at home alone? Sometimes Kevin is! What can you do to survive the times when you're ready to start climbing the walls?

Do you:
A) Take a wild toboggan ride down your stairway, out the front door, and into a snowdrift?
B) Dig through your lousy older brother's stuff and hope that he doesn't notice?
C) Rig up a "firing squad" on the laundry chute?
D) Stare at photos of your family and feel sad?
E) Do something fun that's not dangerous, destructive, or *stupid!?*

Okay, Einstein, what's it gonna be?

Everyone knows that in the movies, they use all sorts of fancy camera angles and editing tricks to make something *look* like something else. Plus, they hire trained people to do stunts like flying down the stairs on a sled.

It's not real, it only *looks* real. Trying that trick (or anything like it) in real life *is really dangerous*. In other words, DON'T TRY IT AT HOME!!!!

If your older brother is like Buzz, choosing answer **B** may also be hazardous to your health. Answer **C** is not too bright (your mom might not be too happy about all those little marks on the wall) and besides, how many people actually have a laundry chute and an air rifle that really work?

Answer **D** says that you stare at photos of your family and feel sad. Forget about it! It may seem like your only option at times, but squelch it. Besides, how long can moping around take? When you're done, you'll still have a lot of time on your hands to feel bored.

So ... you've probably guessed by now that **E** is the correct answer. Good for you. Now, get over being bored. Get busy!

Make a Time Capsule of Yourself

Archaeologists look for clues in things that people wrote, art that they made, and tools they used to find out how people lived and thought in ancient times. Pretend it is the year 3000. What can you leave now for the archaeologists of the future to show them how interesting *you* are?

Make a personal time capsule. You might include:

• An essay, audiotape, or videotape explaining who you are, what your interests are, what you do every day, your favorite foods, and the good things and bad things in the world today. Be sure to give lots of details.

- A list of things that are important to you. Do you have a favorite hat, a book that means a lot to you, or another belonging that tells something about you? Make a list of these things and explain why you like them.
- A history of yourself up until now. What have been the most important events in your life?
- A self-portrait or a photograph.
- A list of five people who have influenced you the most, and why.
- A list of your predictions for the future.

After you have gathered the contents for your time capsule, you'll need to store them. Use a shoe box, a cardboard tube, an egg carton, or a plastic container to make your time capsule. Seal the contents in the container.

Decorate the outside and date it. Put the time capsule in a safe place.

At-Home Fool-the-Eye Stunts

Film directors aren't the only ones who can fool other people. Sure, they have stunt people and special effects. But you can create your own special effects with a few simple magic techniques.

Magic is the art of fooling people. The secret to performing amazing magic tricks is to let your audience see *only* what you want them to see.

How can you learn to "read" your friends' minds, turn water into ice, pull a quarter out of thin air, and other tricks that fool the eye? Practice—while you are at home alone, of course.

Magic Tips

- While you are performing, distract your audience by talking a lot. Take their minds off trying to figure out how you do your trick.
- Practice your tricks in front of a mirror to see how they look.
- Don't perform the same trick twice in a row.
- Don't tell anyone how a trick is done before you do it.

Pull a Coin From a Friend's Ear

- Before you begin, place a coin between your index finger and your middle finger. Push the coin toward the back of your hand, so it doesn't show when you hold up your palm.
- Show your friend your palms quickly and casually. (They will look empty!)
- Say that you can make things appear magically. Reach behind your friend's ear, and curve your fingers so the coin drops between your index finger and thumb.
- Pull out the coin and show it to your friend!

The Disappearing Penny

A penny inside a glass disappears when you say the magic words!

- (Trick: The penny only *looks* like it's in the glass.) Put the penny in the palm of your hand, then place a clear drinking glass, open side up, *over* it. Show your audience, saying that you will make the penny disappear from inside the glass when you say the magic word. (Only *you* know it is not really *inside* the glass.)
- Put a handkerchief over the glass (which is over the penny) and say some magic words. Give the glass (still covered by the handkerchief) to a member of the audience. Ask them to uncover the glass. The penny is gone! (It's hidden in your hand.)

Magic Cubes
You can turn water to ice—instantly!

- Before you perform the trick, tightly pack a Styrofoam or other opaque cup with cotton, tissue, or paper towels, about half-full. Put an ice cube in the cup.
- Have the cup ready, along with another cup containing water. Explain to the audience that you have magical powers to turn water into ice. (Don't let your audience see inside either cup.)
- Pour water into the cup with the padding and ice cube. Pick up the cup and explain to the audience you will use your powers of concentration to turn the water to ice. Tell everyone to think about snow, ice, etc. After a moment, pour the ice cube onto the table! (Trick: The padding will have absorbed the water you poured in.)

Read My Mind

A friend chooses a coin and concentrates on the date. You can tell him what date he's thinking of!

• Choose five coins of equal value (all pennies, for example) but with different mintage dates. (The year stamped onto the coin, for the year it was made.) Put the coins on the table. Turn your back while you ask your friend to choose one and to memorize the date. Have him hold the coin tightly while thinking of the date.

• In the meantime, *you* keep your back turned and pretend to concentrate hard.

• After a minute or two, ask your friend to place the penny (or other type of coin) he chose with the other coins. You pretend to concentrate, while feeling the coins, saying you are "picking up vibrations." You guess the right date! (Trick: The coin that feels the warmest will be the right one! The heat from your friend's hand will have made the coin that he chose warmer than the others.)

A Hole In Your Head?

Can you really push an object through your head and pop it out of your mouth? With this trick you can!

• Before doing the trick, take a small edible object (a grape, a pea, or a piece of candy are all good) and put it in your mouth. While it is in your mouth, take *another* of the same object and hold it up for your audience to see.

Tell them that you have the power to pop it out through your head. (By the way, it takes practice to talk normally with something in your mouth!)

- Quickly toss the object from one hand to the other, telling the audience that the object needs to "warm up."
- Raise your left hand and push down on the top of your head, as if you are pushing the object down into your head.
- Open your mouth—the object pops out! (Trick: Keep the object in your right hand, but pretend to toss it to the left hand. Curve your left hand so it looks like the object is inside it when you push down on your head.)

Oozing Goop

Is it liquid or is it solid? You can make oozing goop that *looks* like liquid but it's actually solid. While this isn't really a magic trick, making oozing goop is a fun way to baffle your friends!

You will need:

- ∗ 3 tablespoons cornstarch (approximately)
- ∗ 3 tablespoons water (approximately)
- ∗ Food coloring, if desired

Put the cornstarch in a small bowl. Slowly add water, mixing constantly. Add food coloring, drop by drop, if you wish. The mixture will thicken and turn shiny. (It takes time, so be patient.) Add more water if the mixture is too thick. Oozing goop looks wet, but hey, it's not!

THERE'S ONLY ONE OF YOU

"Kevin, you're such a disease." "What's the matter with you!?" "You're the only one who has to make trouble." With those kinds of comments, it's no wonder Kevin wants his family to get lost. "Everyone in this family hates me.... I hope I never see any of you jerks again!" he tells them.

Ever feel the way Kevin does? Who doesn't—*sometimes!*

Kevin knows he's not so bad. He proves it when he's at home alone by keeping Marv and Harry from robbing his family's house. He shows everyone that he isn't helpless. Even if you sometimes feel crummy about yourself, *you know* deep down that you're really okay, too.

Remember—you're only as dumb as you feel. Think of five reasons why you're *not* a "disease":

FIVE REASONS WHY I'M NOT A "DISEASE":

1. _____
2. _____
3. _____

4. _____

5. _____

Revenge!!

Okay—you *know* you're not a total zero. Even if people say stupid, insulting things to you, *you* know they're wrong.

But if someone keeps saying nasty things to you, are you just gonna stand there and take it? Are you going to be a wimp? Are you kidding? No way! Tough times call for drastic measures. You've got to fight fire with fire.

Now, that *doesn't* mean that you have to stoop to the level of a jerk. You don't really want to hurt someone badly. (It's no fun, and it will make *you* feel bad!) Still, there *are* ways to answer people when they make you mad.

Sometimes a look is worth a thousand words. Standing in front of a mirror, practice a variety of disgusted looks that can let you answer the stupidest comments without saying a word. Here's how:

The Look That Says...

- "You are *so* boring."—Stare at person, right in the eyes. Yawn loudly in her face.
- "That comment is so stupid and childish, I can't even answer it."—Raise one eyebrow slightly while staring at the person. Look at him as if something green and disgusting is caught between his teeth. Try to look like you feel a little sick, then look away.
- "You're wasting my time."—Roll your eyes, sigh, and look at your watch.

What would you do if you ended up in a big city, all by yourself? Would you ride in a cool, chauffeur-driven limousine?

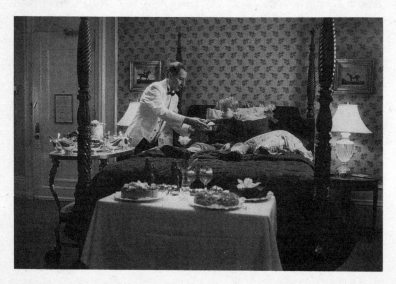

Or would you check into a super-deluxe hotel suite?

- "You are pond scum."—Narrow your eyes and look the person up and down. Stare, with an expression of utter disgust, at one area of his or her face.
- "You are so gross, it's funny."—Look at the person and smile slightly. Then start to giggle softly to yourself. Shake your head if the person asks why you're laughing. Walk away, still giggling.

Ten Snappy Comebacks to Stupid Comments

There are times when you need a snappy comeback to dumb comments. Forget about saying, "I know you are but what am I!?" It's the oldest, tiredest line in the book.

To answer the dumbest of the dumb comments, you need to get creative. Try thinking of some original, snappy putdowns yourself. Or if you're stuck, try one of these:

1. "Boy, *that* comment was witty. Did you stay up all night thinking of it?"

2. "You know, you look more like a rodent every day."

3. "Why don't you go climb back under your rock?"

4. "Did you get up on the wrong side of your web this morning?"

5. "Hey, you're ugly."

6. "Really, you're so funny, you should be on TV."

7. "Woof!"

8. "I'm not going to dignify that stupid comment with an answer."

9. "Can't you think of anything more intelligent to say than *that*?"

10. "Ever consider getting a brain transplant?"

SPECIAL TRAVEL ALERT!!
SURVIVING AWAY FROM HOME

What would *you* do if you ended up in a big city, all by yourself? If you are like Kevin, you would check into a superdeluxe hotel suite, order room service all the time, take in the sights of the city, ride in a cool chauffeur-driven limousine, and go hog-wild at the toy store of your dreams. It sounds like a whole lot more fun than staying with your family at some fleabag motel in the middle of nowhere!!

For a while, Kevin has a great time all alone in New York City. But after a while, he begins to feel lonely and miss his family. And soon, he realizes that his dream vacation could turn into a nightmare if he's not careful. The creepy concierge at the hotel wants to kick Kevin out. Worse, Harry and Marv are on the loose and out for revenge. It seems like *everyone* is after Kevin.

To get out of a lot of sticky situations when he is traveling all by himself, Kevin has to think fast. When the Wet Bandits are chasing him, Marv tells Harry they're sure to catch Kevin. "After all," says Marv, "kids are helpless." Is he ever wrong! ...

Kevin is *not* helpless, even if he is a kid. Using Operation Ho-Ho-Ho, he lures the robbers into a clever trap. He stops Harry and Marv from robbing Mr. Duncan's toy store and stealing the money that is supposed to go to sick children.

Kevin beats Harry and Marv at their own game. Because of his quick wits, the robbers end up being pretty helpless themselves, coated in a sticky mess of glue and birdseed. Harry and Marv look like idiots as they are taken back to jail by the police.

When you are traveling, you don't have to be defenseless either. Even if you don't get the chance to bust crime the way Kevin does when he's out of town, you can still survive in a strange place—without feeling helpless.

Don't take a "backseat" when you're traveling—even if you're stuck in the car with your brother who gets carsick!! Take part in your family's vacation plans—you can learn fun facts about where you're going and know how to get around town once you're there. How do you do it?

First, **PREPARE:** Learn about the place that you are going to visit *before* you leave. Look at a map. How far is the place from your house? Are you going stay in a motel, a hotel, or someone else's house? Write down the name and telephone number of that place.

Remember how Kevin's sister says he's so helpless that he can't even pack for himself? *You* can help pack for yourself. Make sure to bring essentials—toothbrush, a good book to read, underwear, etc.—but don't pack *too* much. Your bag will weigh a ton! (Kevin survives in New York without bringing anything!)

Keep money, cameras, and other valuables close to you when you're traveling. . . .

Next, **GETTING THERE:** Even though Kevin has fun when he's separated from his family, in real life it would be scary and dangerous for you. Don't wander away from your parents in airports, train or bus stations, or anywhere else. Pay attention to where they—and you—are going. Keep track of the bags or other items that you are carrying with you.

When you are **AWAY FROM HOME:** Always carry an emergency quarter and the address and phone number where you are staying. If you are going sightseeing, decide on a place to meet your family if you get separated from them. Again, don't wander away, even if they're driving you crazy! Keep money, cameras, and other valuables close to you.

You already know that you shouldn't accept anything from strangers. Don't follow strangers anywhere by yourself.

IF YOU GET LOST: Don't panic. Instead, try to find a police officer, security guard, or information desk that can help you find your family.

Boredom Busters

Does waiting for trains, planes, and automobiles make you nuts? Do your parents take *forever* getting ready to go out? Try these ways to make passing time more fun:

- If you're in a public place like an airport or train station, take a look at the people around you. Is the guy with the funny haircut really a spy? Is the woman wearing all that jewelry really a famous movie star? Make up stories about the people you see.

- Keep a travel journal, and write in it when you're bored. Write down details about all the things, places, and people you see. Did you try new kinds of food that day? See something super-weird? Sometimes writing it down can help you remember your trip even better than photographs can!

- Bring a book about the place you're visiting and read about the places you are going to see. (You will sound like a real expert to your family if you recite little-known facts at the right time!!)

- Kevin has a ball using his father's credit card when he's traveling. But *everyone* knows that sooner or later, you really have to *pay* for all the things that you pay for with "plastic." Kids can't get credit cards, but you *can* set up a "credit card" system with your friends for favors. Figure out who you want in your "credit card" club, and design an official card. (You can even have it coated in plastic if you want!) Tell your friends all about it when you get home from your trip.

- Bring a book of lists, *The Guiness Book of World Records*, or anything else that might hold your interest for a while. Do you know the world's record for jumping on a pogo stick? For eating hot dogs? Do you know how much the fattest cat in the world weighed? You can learn!

BEING SMART AT BEING ALONE
BY KEVIN McCALLISTER

So ... you've read all about me and the things that I did when I was all alone. You've learned some way cool things about what to do if you're bored out of your skull, found out how to handle your brother or sister when they're making you crazy, and learned some excellent snappy comebacks to rat-face comments. I wish I had had this book when *I* was at home alone!

Oh, yeah—you also read about how to get home without getting lost, kidnapped, or run over, learned about how to deal with strangers on the phone or at the door, and worked on ways to get rid of creepy feelings while you are at home by yourself. And don't forget the stuff about surviving being alone when you're *away from home.*

As you know by now, being at home alone is as serious as it is fun. I had a great time when I spent time by myself, even though a lot of crazy things happened to me. And I think you will too.

Surviving when you're alone—at home or away—is not tough. Take it from me. I know, I've been there. All you have to do is USE YOUR BRAIN. Use common sense. Don't be a goof and do really dangerous stuff.

I know, I know. You're saying, why is *Kevin* saying this stuff? He does plenty of stupid things and nothing really bad happens to him! And you're right. But that's because I'm in a *movie!!*

In *real* life, doing crazy things is a lot more dangerous than in the movies. But in real life, you can stay safe and still have as much fun as I do. And that's the trick to surviving at home alone, isn't it?

SO DON'T BE A DISEASE. HAVE A GREAT TIME!!

I had a great time when I spent time by myself, even though a lot of crazy things happpened to me. And I think you will too.